Bible Treasure Hunt

Bible Treasure Hunt

An Interactive Bible-Lands
Adventure Story

C.W. MICHAELS

BARBOUR
PUBLISHING

© 2010 by Barbour Publishing, Inc.

Created in cooperation with Snapdragon Group℠, Tulsa, Oklahoma, USA.

ISBN 978-1-60260-834-4

Published by Barbour Publishing, Inc., P.O. Box 719, Uhrichsville, Ohio 44683, www.barbourbooks.com

Our mission is to publish and distribute inspirational products offering exceptional value and biblical encouragement to the masses.

Member of the
Evangelical Christian
Publishers Association

Printed in the United States of America.

For Brett

Faith isn't the ability to believe long
and far into the misty future.
It's simply taking God at His Word
and taking the next step.

JONI EARECKSON TADA

Contents

Contents

Prologue

I was standing behind a tall shelf of books, peering through a narrow opening, pretending to spy on an old man shelving books on the other side.

"Is there something I can help you with, young man?" he said suddenly, catching me off guard. So much for a career in espionage.

Surprised that he spoke English, I walked down the aisle without responding and poked my head around the corner. The old man lowered his thick, black-rimmed glasses, and our eyes met. He beckoned to me with a long finger.

I gulped as I moved toward him.

"May I ask what you're doing down here?" he asked. "Why are you spying on me?"

"I was bored," I answered, my voice sounding small and mousy. "I just wanted to see what was down here, that's all."

Then in a flash I knew what his next question was going to be, and I hurried to form a reasonable reply.

"You didn't see the sign?" he asked.

"Oh, the sign," I said, trying to sound more confident. On my way down to this room I had passed a sign that indicated the area was private. "It's written in Hebrew, and we just moved here from America." I didn't lie to him. I *did* see the sign, and it *was* written in Hebrew. Of course I didn't exactly tell the truth either. I still needed some help perfecting the Hebrew dialect, but I could read the language and comprehend it quite well.

The old man gave me a strange look, his thick eyebrows furrowing above his glasses. He didn't say anything for what seemed like an hour, and then he introduced himself.

"I'm Dr. Oliver Manning. What's your name?"

"My name's Brett. Brett Sanger."

"Sanger. Elizabeth Sanger's child?"

I nodded.

"I haven't had the pleasure of meeting your

mother yet, but I've been told she's a top-notch librarian. Do you like books?" he asked.

I hesitated for a moment, deciding whether to once again tell a half truth.

I chose to be honest. "No. Not really."

"Well then, Mr. Sanger, do you like adventure?"

I shrugged. "Yeah, I guess."

Dr. Manning paused to take another long, hard look at me. "I see," he said, "but what if I had a book full of adventure that might interest even a boy like you?" His eyes grew dark and his eyebrows drew together, his tone serious. "Are you courageous?"

"Yes, sir," I said, trying to hide the fact that his sudden transformation was a little frightening.

"Good." I expected more to follow but that was it. He proceeded to remove a ring full of keys from his side.

His sudden transformation was a little frightening.

"You must turn your back, close your eyes, and promise not to open them," he said.

Without hesitating, I turned away from him and closed my eyes. I heard his keys jingle and the sound of wood touching the concrete floor. Maybe it was the painting I'd noticed hanging on the wall. Then I could hear a key being wedged into a lock. Hinges squeaked as a door was opened. Before long, the door was shut again, locked, and the painting apparently replaced.

"Okay. You can open your eyes and turn around," he told me.

I did as he said.

"Now follow me."

I followed the old man down a long aisle lined with rows of bookshelves. We turned right down one of the rows and then left, stopping at an old olive wood door, which the doctor unlocked. The door sounded like it hadn't been opened in a very long time.

Everything in the room was covered in dust.

"Wait here."

I watched as he felt his way down the center of the room and disappeared from sight. A faint light began to flicker from a single bulb in the middle of the room, and a chain hanging from the ceiling swayed, casting a thin, moving shadow on the wall. Everything in the room was covered in dust, and cobwebs grew everywhere.

"Over here," he said.

I swept my arms through the air as I walked, knocking down the cobwebs the doctor had parted moments earlier.

When I reached him, the old man was inserting a long, rusty key into a large trunk that looked like a treasure chest. As he lifted the lid, dust rose and settled on the books inside. Dr. Manning removed the largest one and held it up for me to see.

The first thing I noticed was that the spine was beyond repair and the pages were tattered and thin. The gold lettering was chipped and uneven, but the indentation on the leather cover clearly identified the title: *Bible Treasure Hunt*. The volume was massive compared to the chapter books I was sometimes forced to read, yet as the doctor opened it up and began to carefully turn the brittle pages, blowing each page clean, its painted pictures, glorious and heroic, somehow made me feel like I was part of the story.

He closed the book and handed it to me. Then he lowered the chest's lid and pulled the chain dangling below the dusty bulb. We slowly made our way out of the dark room.

Chapter 1

A Long, Boring Day

I never would have had a peek at that strange book if my dad hadn't injured his knee while pulling down an offensive rebound. My dad's name is Josh Sanger. You may have heard of him; he played six years for the Phoenix Suns, making a living mixing it up in-

He played six years for the Phoenix Suns.

side the paint, wrestling the ball from the likes of Shaquille O'Neal and Kevin Garnett, throwing fireballs down court to Steve Nash for easy buckets.

Knee injuries are career killers in the NBA. At least my dad's was. He had surgery and spent a year rehabbing it, but he'd lost a little both horizontally and vertically. The Suns released him, and two days later he received a call from the Hapoel Jerusalem basketball team of the Israeli League. One week later we were on a plane traveling halfway around the world to our new home in Jerusalem, Israel.

For many kids my age, the suddenness of it all might have created a meltdown. But for me it was like moving to the other side of town. I was born in Cremona in Northern Italy, where my dad began his professional basketball career. When I was four, he was traded to the Aris team in Greece. A few years later, an NBA scout discovered him and we were on our way to the United States.

Going back to Israel was actually a homecoming for my parents. They were both born in Tel Aviv, high school sweethearts who married a few weeks after my dad signed to play pro ball in Italy. I not only speak English, but Italian, Greek, and Hebrew as well. So like I said, moving to

I had plenty of time to explore and check out my new surroundings.

Israel was like moving across town for me. Both sets of grandparents and my aunts and uncles all lived within thirty minutes of the condo we bought in Jerusalem.

The best thing of all was that the beginning of the new school year was still four weeks away, which meant I had plenty of time to explore and check out my new surroundings.

As it turned out, I only had to go to one place to discover adventure, and it just so happened to be the first place I visited.

On our first morning in Jerusalem, my dad was eager to get to the arena and meet his new teammates. And so was I. When school was out, I lived at the gym. I had inherited many of my dad's physical characteristics— a long nose and fairly large ears—and I was

When school was out, I lived at the gym.

tall and unusually quick for a twelve-year-old. More than anything, I loved to compete. But unfortunately, the first workout was more of a meet-and-greet and strategy session. This was one practice I would have to sit out.

My mom, on the other hand, was built like a porcelain tea cup, a tea cup that I drank very little from. I inherited her small chin, fair skin, and quiet personality, but her love of books swept right past me. She spent many hours with me sharing her passion for books, reading one after another to me, while I envisioned myself dribbling a basketball, building a fort, playing a video; in other words, doing anything other than sitting and listening to my mom read a book out loud.

So when my dad told me that I would be spending the day with my mom at the library, my head dropped. My attitude would have put off most moms, but mine saw it as a challenge, an opportunity to sharpen her storytelling skills. As we walked she described the building we were soon to enter. She knew that Batman was my favorite superhero, so she described an ancient build-ing like one you might find in Gotham City: a building with

It was going to be a long, boring day.

palace doors and the hushed silence of a game of hide-and-seek; a building whose walls held the key to one's imagination, filled with mystery, intrigue, and wisdom; a building filled with books just waiting to be held and cherished. And that's where she lost me.

She could tell my mind had drifted else-where.

"Just give it a chance," she said, "for me."

I nodded my head to appease her, but I was

practically positive it wouldn't do any good. It was going to be a long, boring day.

Chapter 2

A Treasure Beyond
Comprehension

I carried the book back to where Dr. Manning and I met, and Dr. Manning laid the rusty key on the table that separated us.

"The book you are holding is a treasure beyond comprehension," he said, "passed down to me by my father-in-law. It is literally a window to the past."

"Okaaaay." *What history book isn't?* I thought to myself.

My skeptical tone didn't escape him. "I don't think you understand. That book doesn't just teach you history; it pulls you into it. It's a secret passage, a hidden door, a revolving bookcase. It warms you and cools you down. It lifts your hair and rains down on you. It is the adventure of another lifetime; a roller coaster that continues when the track ends; a book that is most certainly not for the faint of heart. So, what do you say? Do you possess the courage necessary to open it up and take the ride?"

"What you're saying doesn't make a whole lot of sense."

I didn't say anything at first. I just let it soak in for a moment. None of what he was saying could be true. This book didn't have plug-ins or space for batteries.

"Well, are you up for the adventure?"

I decided to just humor him. "Sure, what do I do?" I asked, smirking.

"Don't mock me, boy! If you don't believe the book can do anything for you, it won't and you'll be wasting my time."

"You have to admit," I said, "what you're saying doesn't make a whole lot of sense."

"You mean to say that it's not reasonable?"

I nodded, holding up the book with both hands so that it didn't fall apart. "It's made of paper and leather," I said very matter-of-factly.

"Oh, but it's so much more. You just have to have faith."

"Okay, so say I believe. How do I make it work?"

"We'll get to that in a moment. Before I explain the intricacies of the book, you must promise to fulfill just one request."

"What's that?" I asked.

"You must agree to take someone along on your adventures."

"Huh?" I grunted, looking around and seeing no one.

"My granddaughter," Dr. Manning continued.

Again my eyes scanned the room. "Your granddaughter?"

Then it hit me. Not only was he suggesting I go on some mysterious adventure connected with the tattered old book in my hands, he wanted me to take a girl along. *No way; no how. I just got here*, I thought. I certainly wasn't going to spend time with some girl, especially one I'd never met. I needed to find someone I could shoot baskets with. Someone I could throw a football to. Girls played with each others' hair and went to the mall. The old man was crazy if he thought I was going to spend the remainder of my summer with some girl.

I was just about to tell him all this and be

on my way when the prettiest girl I'd ever seen walked around the corner.

"This is the last of the books, Grandpa."

She stopped when she saw me. "Hello," she said.

The doctor cut in. "Gabriella, this is Brett. Brett, this is my granddaughter, Gabriella."

My heart started beating really fast, and my "hi" came out sounding squashed.

"So what do you say, Brett? Should I take your silence as a yes?"

I nodded agreeably, though I couldn't remember the question.

"What's going on, Grandpa? You have that look in your eye."

He shrugged. "What look?"

Idiot,
I thought to myself.

"That look that you get when you have just gotten your way." She turned to me. "I go by Gabby."

Without thinking I said, "I go by Brett." *Idiot*, I thought to myself.

Gabby laughed. "You're funny," she said.

"Young Brett here just moved into town, and he's looking for adventure."

Gabby stared down at the book I was holding and quickly turned to her grandfather.

"You mean"—her mouth dropped open—"he's the one?"

They both looked at me. *The one what?* I asked myself before saying the words out loud.

The blue in her eyes turned turquoise and began to sparkle. "You mean I finally get to experience it?" she said.

Her grandfather nodded and she ran to him, wrapped her arms around his waist, and buried her head in his chest.

I watched as they embraced each other, the doctor's face full of joy.

Gabby let go and approached me. "Thank you," she said, and to my astonishment she kissed me on the cheek, her long brown hair falling on my shoulders, the scent of vanilla surrounding me. Adventure or no adventure, I knew right then that I would welcome spending time around *this* girl.

Chapter 3

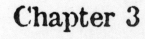

David and Goliath

The next morning my dad woke me up early. "Okay, buddy. I cleared it with the coach. You can hang out at our practice today. Get dressed; we're leaving in ten minutes."

The fact that I didn't budge alarmed my father. Normally I would have hit the ceiling and been searching for my gym shorts before he was halfway out of the room.

"Are you all right?" he asked.

This was a very good question and one I didn't have a good answer for.

> ***The fact that I didn't budge alarmed my father.***

Saying yes would have been admitting I understood why I wanted to spend the day at the library with Gabby rather than at the gym with my dad, which to be honest I didn't yet fully understand. Saying no would have required me to explain all this to my father. So I simply said, "I think I'll go with Mom again this morning in case she needs help with anything at the library."

I actually found myself considering what I should wear.

Dad looked surprised by my answer, and I couldn't blame him because so was I.

He examined me closely. "Hmm," he said, "you look like my son; you sound like my son. What year were you born?"

"Dad—"

"What year?"

I sighed. "Nineteen ninety-seven."

"What was the name of your first basketball team?"

"The Lakers. Come on, Dad, it's me."

"All right, just making sure." He looked at his watch. "I need to make some coffee and then get going. Have fun at the library, and I'll see you tonight."

I couldn't fall back asleep so I decided to take a shower and get dressed for the day. I actually found myself considering what I should wear. Usually I'd have just grabbed the first thing

I saw. It wouldn't have mattered if it was clean or dirty or if I'd worn it the day before. Then again, I had never tried to impress anyone. In the course of eighteen hours my whole outlook had changed.

My mom and I arrived at the library before normal visiting hours. I decided I would hang upstairs for a little while, feeling nervous about going down to the basement. So you can imagine my surprise when Gabby appeared out of nowhere.

"Good morning," she said, and then walked right past me and introduced herself to my mom.

Gabby reached for my hand and I cautiously accepted.

"You want to go downstairs?" she asked, turning from my mother to me with a smile on her face and a twinkle in her eyes.

I looked at my mom. "Go ahead," she said, a small smile curling one side of her mouth. She'd always been able to see right through me. I turned away from her, pretending not to notice her reaction.

Gabby reached for my hand and I cautiously accepted. I was pretty sure I'd never met anyone like her. As we turned left at the base of the stairs, I could see that the book was no longer where I left it.

"Good morning, Brett," Dr. Manning said without looking up from the weathered scroll he was studying that was spread out across the table. "Are you ready to hear how the book works?"

I had decided before I arrived at the library that I would play along since Gabby was so excited. But I still wasn't close to buying into the idea. I mean, come on, a book that could physically transport a person back

There was that word again: **faith**.

in time? I had never claimed to be the smartest person alive, but I knew enough not to believe in fairy tales.

I didn't want Gabby to be upset, though, so I replied, "Yes, sir. I'm ready."

Dr. Manning began by telling us that we needed to be very careful with the book because it was so fragile. He would be the only one to handle it from now on. Gabby was fully absorbed in what he was saying. I couldn't stop staring at her. He then told us that there were only two requirements to initiating the process. First, we must have faith. There was that word again: *faith*. How could I have faith in something that was impossible? And second, for the

book to work we had to be at the actual location
where the event took place. That was it. Oh, and
to fit into our surroundings, it was important
that we dress in the attire of the day. I thought
this would get me out of it since I wasn't exactly
dressed for Bible times.

I pointed to myself and smiled at Dr. Manning.

"No need to worry about the clothes, Brett,"
he responded. Then he removed a long yellowed
T-shirt from a dusty cardboard box. "This should
fit you. I wore this on the adventures when I was
your age." He handed me the garment. "And
here is a tunic and a pair of sandals. There's a
bathroom around the corner."

"You want me to put this stuff on now?" I
asked in amazement.

"Of course. Your first adventure begins this
morning."

"Seriously? But wait. . .I gotta ask—why
me?"

"Didn't you tell me you were bored?" he said, leaning toward me.

"Of course. Your first adventure begins this morning."

"Yeah, sure
. . .but what if I hadn't said that? Would you still

have chosen me?"

"Yes."

"Why? There are a thousand Jewish boys my age in this city."

He removed his glasses and set them down on the table. "My father-in-law chose me long before I married his daughter, and he told me that it was my job to pass the book on. I asked him whom I should pass it to and he said I would know the moment I looked into the person's eyes. I have looked into thousands of eyes over the past fifty years but have seen nothing. I began to question whether I was discerning enough. And then yesterday you walked around the corner and our eyes met. I knew instantly that you were the one I'd been waiting for."

I have to admit that though I was still skeptical of the whole thing, it was kind of cool being "the one." Without another word, I headed for the bathroom and got dressed. The yellowed cotton shirt was like a gown, the base of it covering my knees. I wasn't sure what I was supposed to do with the blanket thing he called a tunic. The sandals were thin and had straps that wrapped around my ankles like a vine. I felt like an idiot when I reappeared, and Gabby's giggling sure didn't help.

"Excellent," the doctor said. Hardly the word

I would have used. "You'll need this also," he said as he approached me and wrapped a piece of rope around my waist. He took the tunic from me, folded it lengthwise, and then slung it over my shoulder.

"My turn," Gabby said and rushed off toward the bathroom.

"I trust you will take good care of her," the doctor said once she was out of sight.

"Yes, sir. I won't let anything happen to her," I said, trying hard to sound confident.

"You still don't believe, do you?"

"I'd like to. It's just. . .I don't know. . .so unreasonable."

His warm smile surprised me. "Ah, unreasonable. I completely agree."

His surrender caught me off guard. "You do?"

"I do." He paused, carefully studying me. "Do you believe in God, Brett?"

I nodded.

"Do you think that believing in God is reasonable?"

I had never thought of God in such terms before.

"Have you ever seen God? Have you ever touched God? Have you ever heard His voice?"

I shook my head.

"But you believe. You have unreasonable

faith that God exists. This book works the same way. You must have unreasonable faith."

I could hear Gabby's footsteps as she approached us. She was bubbling with excitement. Her clothes were much like mine but with a feminine touch. She looked beautiful.

"I'd like to take a picture of the two of you together," the doctor said, and before I could respond, Gabby had her arm around me, her head leaning against my shoulder. "Say cheese."

Dr. Manning had no trouble getting permission from my mom to take me on a day trip. Come to find out, he was somewhat of a legend. He had spent fifty years as an archaeologist and was renowned for his biblical discoveries and writings on ancient antiquities. My mom had read several of his books and was a big fan. So when he asked permission to take me to the Valley of Elah—just outside of Jerusalem—not only did she consent, she thanked him profusely.

Dr. Manning had a sweet ride: a 1935 Bentley in beautiful condition. It was gray with a black interior. The only drawback was that it had no horsepower. Not that it mattered since we cruised along at five miles below the speed limit. There was one plus to this, though: it gave Gabby plenty of time to tell me the story we were about to experience—the battle between the simple sheepherder, David, and the merciless giant, Goliath. I knew the gist of the story but none of the small details. For a twelve-year-old, Gabby was an excellent storyteller, and though I hated to admit it to myself, I was actually beginning to get excited.

When we arrived at the scene of the battle, I was a little disappointed. Gabby's story had been so animated that I actually expected the hills to be full of soldiers. Instead, I saw two hills facing each other, with a creek bed winding away between them.

The doctor walked in front of us carrying the book. We followed him in silence until he sat down on a large rock and invited us to do the same.

Though I hated to admit it to myself, I was actually beginning to get excited.

"There is one more thing you must know, Brett. Once you step back in time, you will recall nothing about the time you are entering. The battle will be as new to you as it is to the soldiers who are engaged in it. Neither you nor Gabby will have any recollection of the story that she just told you."

"How will we get back?" I asked.

"The travel time is precisely one hour. Not a minute less, not a minute more. Remember, son: unreasonable faith."

I nodded.

"Okay, you two. You are about to experience an adventure of a lifetime, an adventure upon which no monetary value could ever be placed. For in this adventure, the treasure isn't merely silver and gold, it is history in action. When the Lord invited King Solomon to ask for anything he wanted, Solomon didn't ask for riches or a long life; he asked for wisdom. And because Solomon asked for this, the Lord not only granted him wisdom but riches as well."

"Where are we?" I said to Gabby.

I was beginning to get a little nervous, which actually felt good. My dad once told me that to perform well in life it's important to be a little nervous. He said nerves are a sign that you're focused and taking the task at hand seriously.

The doctor began to open the book and turn the pages. "Remember," he said, "unreasonable faith." I closed my eyes and tried to relax. Then for the first time, I let myself believe.

"You can open your eyes," he said.

When I did he was gone, and Gabby and I were standing in the middle of a bunch of soldiers.

"Where are we?" I said to Gabby.

She shook her head. "I don't know."

Suddenly there was a loud cry—so loud that Gabby and I grabbed each other and held on tight. Slowly we turned to see where it was coming from. At the top of the hill across from us stood a humongous man, bigger than anyone I had ever seen. He wore a bronze helmet and bronze armor, and a long spear was slung on his back. When he shouted his voice was like a lion's roar. The soldiers standing around us looked shaken by the giant's menacing roar. Mostly they just stared, but a few were glancing behind them to try to determine the reaction of a man, dressed for battle and wearing a crown. I assumed he was the king—but he looked just as scared as they did.

I reached up and tugged at the garment of the soldier standing closest to me. When he looked down, I asked, "What's going on?" When he looked at me curiously, I repeated my question in Hebrew.

"What do you mean what's going on? Goliath's been taking his stand every morning and every evening now for forty days. And what is she doing here?" he asked. "This is no place for children, let alone young ladies. Get back to the camp."

We might have been convinced to go if we had known where the camp was. Instead, I dropped down behind a nearby rock and pulled Gabby down beside me.

We had been there only a few minutes when we saw a boy approach from the far side. He was maybe a year or two older than me. He was carrying loaves of bread and blocks of cheese, and he stopped very near where we were crouched down. "So are we winning?" he asked, his voice giving us both a start.

"I don't know. Who are *we*?" I asked.

"Well, Hebrews, of course."

"It would appear that the other side has a giant," I said. "A *mad* giant, who is insisting that someone come out and fight him. One of the soldiers told me he's been roaring for forty days and no one has yet gone up against him."

My words appeared to anger the boy. "We'll see about that!" he said, rushing off. He gave the food to a man in a nearby tent and then pushed his way through the crowd of soldiers until he spotted who he was looking for. He appeared to be arguing with several other

"So are we winning?" he asked.

men for some time.

Suddenly there was another loud shout. "Why do you come out and line up for battle?" the giant yelled. "Am I not a Philistine, and are you not the servants of Saul? Choose a man and have him come down to me. If he is able to fight and kill me, we will become your subjects; but if I overcome him and kill him, you will become our subjects and serve us." He looked around at the soldiers standing beside him, shook his head, and bent over, placing his hands on his knees and letting out a deafening belly laugh. He straightened up and bellowed, "This day I defy the ranks of Israel! Give me a man and let us fight each other." The soldiers behind the giant joined in, laughing and pointing at our soldiers.

"Give me a man and let us fight each other."

Gabby and I looked around to see who would go out to meet the giant, but no man seemed willing to step forward. We heard the soldiers talking among themselves about how the king would give great wealth to the man who killed the giant, but that wouldn't mean much if they were dead.

It was then that we noticed the boy we saw earlier making his way toward the king.

"Come on, Gabby," I said. "Let's get closer so we can hear what they're saying."

"Let no one lose heart on account of this Philistine," the boy said to the king. "Your servant will go and fight him."

I couldn't believe what my ears were hearing. The boy was my size! The giant was almost twice as tall as him and about five times as thick.

The king replied, "You are not able to go out against this Philistine and fight him; you are only a boy, and he has been a fighting man from his youth."

That didn't deter the boy. "Don't worry," he said. "I know how to fight. Your servant has been keeping his father's sheep. When a lion or a bear

The giant was almost twice as tall as him and about five times as thick.

comes and tries to carry off a sheep from the flock, I go after it, strike it down, and take the sheep from its mouth. Though I'm young, I've done it many times. This uncircumcised Philistine will be like one of them, because he has defied the armies of the living God. The Lord will deliver me from the hand of this Philistine."

To our surprise, the king said, "You are but a

boy. What will your family think of this?"

The boy answered that his mother was dead, his father old, and he had spoken with his brothers, who were nearby serving in the king's army.

With that, the king said, "Go, and the Lord be with you."

We couldn't believe our eyes as the boy made his way down the hill to the riverbed below. Someone in the crowd said the boy was David, the son of Jesse. We could hear several of the soldiers calling him by name and insisting that he get back up the hill. "David," they shouted, "are you insane? What will we tell our father when we carry your dead body back home?"

David wore no armor and carried no sword. A leather pouch was draped across his chest. In his hand he held a shepherd's staff and a sling. He stepped into the stream at the base of the hill. He walked along slowly, reaching down from time to time to pick up a stone, examine it, and place it in his pouch. Finally, he turned and headed in the direction of the Philistine.

Goliath didn't notice David at first. He was still busy laughing and pointing with his comrades. But when he did finally notice the boy, he just stood and stared. Then he walked toward David, his shield bearer scaling the hill a few steps ahead of him. When he and his shield bearer were a short distance from David, the giant realized that he was just a boy and he began to curse and shout.

"Are you serious? You are sending a child to fight me with sticks and stones? Come on, you little runt. I'll tear you apart with my bare hands."

But David didn't even look scared. "Come on after me with your sword and spear and javelin. I come in the name of the Lord Almighty, the God of the armies of Israel. He's on our side, and this day He is going to hand you over to me. I'm going to strike you down and cut off your head!"

Angered by David's words, the giant began to move toward the young sheepherder. David dropped his staff and ran toward him. As he ran, he reached into his pouch, grabbed a stone, and in one motion loaded the stone into the sling. David swung the stone in circles above his head. The stone flew out of the sling too fast for our eyes to see and then raced like a bullet toward the Philistine, embedding itself in

A mighty roar of disbelief went up on both sides of the riverbed.

his enormous forehead. Suddenly Goliath jerked to a stop, his eyes rolled back, and he fell forward, causing the ground to shake as he landed.

A mighty roar of disbelief went up on both sides of the riverbed.

When David reached Goliath, he took the giant's sword, and with his hands held high, he brought it down hard, piercing the Philistine's body. Then pulling up the sword, he brought it down once again, cutting off the giant's head as he said he would. David stood victoriously, holding up Goliath's head by the hair for all to see. The Philistines turned and ran, and with a loud shout the Israelites pursued them and attacked them.

In the meantime, David made his way back up the hill carrying the Philistine's head in his right hand and his sword in his left. He carried the head all the way to the king.

"You can open your eyes now," I said to Gabby, who had stopped watching when David removed the giant's sword, quite confident that David would fulfill his promise to the king.

And then, without warning, everyone was gone, and only Gabby's grandpa stood before us.

Chapter 4

Moses Parts the Sea

I couldn't sleep that night. Who could after experiencing what I had experienced that day? Mom and Dad asked why I was so quiet at dinner, but I couldn't tell them, not yet. I could barely grasp it myself. I had literally traveled three thousand years back in time and stood on an ancient battlefield, watching a young boy kill a fierce giant. When we had returned to Dr. Manning sitting alone in the deserted valley, Gabby and I could barely look at each other. On the way home, Dr.

I had literally traveled three thousand years back in time.

Manning asked if we would like to go on another adventure the next day. Gabby and I looked up wide-eyed, but we both said yes. We rode in silence the rest of the way. Then Gabby hugged me and whispered that she would see me tomorrow.

Once again my dad woke me up early; and once again I told him that I wanted to go to the library instead of basketball practice. He mentioned something about taking my temperature, but my mom said the thermometer was in an unpacked box and she didn't know which one.

"Only one of the coolest miracles ever!"

This time when we arrived at the library I went straight down to the basement, grabbed my garments and sandals, and showed up for duty.

Dr. Manning and Gabby were impressed. In fact, Gabby wasn't even ready to go yet.

"Where are we off to today?" I said.

"The Red Sea," Dr. Manning answered.

"What's at the Red Sea?"

"What's at the Red Sea?" Gabby asked, clearly perplexed by my lack of Bible history knowledge. "Only one of the coolest miracles *ever!*"

Once again my mom was all too willing to send me off with a man she hardly knew. Not that I was complaining; it was certainly working in my favor. And once again Gabby filled me in on every detail of what we were about to experience, although we both realized that neither of us would remember any of it once we stepped back in time.

It was a long drive to the Red Sea, so I heard the story twice this time, which was okay by me since Gabby did such a good job telling it.

When we arrived at the water's edge, Dr. Manning motioned for us to have a seat. He began to flip through the pages. That's when it dawned on me. I was surprised I hadn't thought of it sooner.

"Wait," I said. "What happens if we don't return? Is that possible?"

Dr. Manning answered the first part of the question with: "That's never happened, so there is no need to worry about it."

Okay, I thought to myself, *I guess I can buy that.*

The second part was a little tougher to swallow. "Yes, it is possible to never return. If the book were to be closed before the hour is up, you would be stuck until it is reopened to that page. The one positive with that is that it doesn't have to be reopened in the

> **"Yes, it is possible to never return."**

same location. It can be reopened anywhere and you would return. But like I said, not to worry; I have everything covered. For one thing, I'm here to make sure the book is not closed. And if for some reason or another something happened to me, Gabby's mother knows where you are and what to do."

If I knew then what I know now, that moment would have marked the end of my time travels. But I was young and naïve and never fathomed the worst might actually happen.

"Are you ready?" Dr. Manning asked.

Gabby and I looked at each other and nodded.

"Okay. See you both in an hour."

Suddenly someone crashed into us. "Ouch!" Abby cried.

"Hey!" I hollered. Sprawled out on the ground next to us were a man and woman who'd fallen when they bumped into us.

"So sorry," the man said. "I didn't see you two sitting there."

"So sorry," the man said. "I didn't see you two sitting there."

"Nor I," said the lady.

"That's okay," I said. "We haven't been here

for long. What's going on?" Looking around, I saw that there were thousands of people camped near a huge lake.

"I beg your pardon?" the man said, looking at me as if I had two heads.

"Why are there so many people?" I asked. "This must be some kind of hot spot, huh?"

"Hot spot? I do not understand. We have all fled from Egypt. . .from Pharaoh. We were slaves. Don't you remember?"

I looked at Gabby and we both shrugged.

Suddenly someone near us shouted, "It's the Egyptians! They are pursuing us."

All around us people cried out, "Lord, save us!"

"What's happening?" Gabby asked.

I pointed. "Look, way out in the distance." We could barely see them. Chari-

"This must be some kind of hot spot, huh?"

ots and horsemen, sitting there waiting for us to turn back toward them. A man about twenty feet away yelled, "Moses!" and then another yelled it, and then another.

"Who's Moses?" I said to Gabby.

A man with long white hair and a long white beard, carrying a tall wooden staff, made his way through the crowd. He had to be the guy whose name everyone was yelling.

A man stepped forward and faced Moses. "Was it because there were no graves in Egypt that you brought us to the desert to die?" he demanded.

Another man yelled, "What have you done to us by bringing us out of Egypt? Didn't we say to you in Egypt, 'Leave us alone; let us serve the Egyptians'? It would have been better for us to serve the Egyptians than to die in the desert!"

I felt bad for Moses. Everyone was ganging up on the poor guy.

He raised his arms for everyone to be quiet and said, "Don't be afraid. The Lord will fight for us."

A man and woman near us began arguing with one another. The woman said, "What are we going to do? There is no place for us to go. The sea is on one side and the Egyptians are on the other."

"We need to listen to Moses; the Lord will take care of us," the man said.

"But how do you know?" she responded.

The words came out of my mouth before my mind could register what I was saying: "Unreasonable faith."

"What?" the lady said.

"You must have unreasonable faith that the Lord will take care of us."

I grabbed Gabby's hand. "Come on. We need to follow Moses. He is the Lord's messenger."

We pushed our way through the crowd until we were at the edge of the water, standing beside Moses. To my surprise, he asked me to hold the sack he was carrying. The contents made a clicking noise.

"What do you think is in there?" Gabby said.

"I don't know."

"Bones," said a man near me.

"Excuse me?" I said.

The man's voice was like Darth Vader's. "Bones; the bones of Joseph."

I extended my arm, holding the sack and its contents away from my

The man's voice was like Darth Vader's.

body. "May I ask why Moses would be carrying a man's bones around?"

"Because before he died, Joseph made the sons of Israel promise to carry his bones out of Egypt when God delivered them from the hands of the Egyptians."

The whole bones thing creeped me out. I was just about to hand the sack back to Moses with a weak "no, thank you" when he suddenly raised his staff and stretched his hand over the water. Now pay close attention because what I am about to tell you will sound completely insane, but it is the absolute truth. The water leaped into the air like a blazing fire and spread apart, forming two walls. And then it just stayed there, suspended in air. Everyone started to run through the middle of it. Yes, you heard me right: People were crossing the sea like it was a hundred-meter dash. The ground was bone-dry. It was like an alley between two buildings, only the buildings were made of water and the alley was as wide as a football field. Gabby and I didn't wait for an invitation. We started hoofing it, and I have to say, man, can Gabby run. She began to pull ahead of me (something I've never admitted to anyone until now) when all of a sudden she came to a grinding halt. There was an older man lying on the ground. It looked like he had been trampled and was trying without success to stand up.

"We have to help him," Gabby said.

I knelt down beside the man. It was difficult to hear him with people running and shouting on every side. But we finally realized the man had injured his ankle. He thought it might be broken. I handed off the bag of bones to a man running by, then helped the old man to his feet. He swung one arm around my neck and the other around Gabby's, and we moved forward.

"We have to hurry," I said.

We lost track of time as we labored to keep the injured man on his feet. We were quickly falling to the back of the pack. Then we heard horses' hooves *clip-clopping* behind us. The squeaking wheels of the chariots were gaining on us.

One hundred yards to go. We were now dead last, a good twenty yards behind the last Israelite. I heard a soldier yell, "Get them!"

I wasn't going to risk Gabby's life.

I knew that if we released the man, we could make it to the other side before the Egyptians did, but I would have rather died than do such a thing. I wasn't going to risk Gabby's life, though, so I stopped abruptly.

"What are you doing?" Gabby yelled as I picked the man up into my arms.

"Run!" I yelled.

Her eyes were filled with fear.

"Run, Gabby! Run!"

She turned and ran and my heart relaxed a little. The old man and I were twenty yards away from the finish line when the Egyptians caught up with us; the lead horse was now parallel with us. The chariot driver snarled at me. *Unreason-able faith*, I told myself and kept walking. I knew that if I had unreasonable faith that the Lord would save me, then He would.

Suddenly the chariot began to fall back. I kept moving the best I could, though I was really tired by that point. Ten more feet. . .five

We had the best seats in the house, right behind Moses.

. . .I finally reached the other side and lowered the man to the ground. Several men stepped forward to help us; one carried the injured man away with him.

I turned around to see the Egyptian chariots ramming into each other like bumper cars, and I heard an Egyptian soldier yell, "Let's get away from the Israelites! The Lord is fighting for them against Egypt."

We had the best seats in the house, right behind Moses. As he continued to hold his rod in the air, the water on the far side came crashing down with a roar. The Egyptians closest to us turned back in panic as the walls of water fell on them, splashing down like elephants doing cannonballs, overpowering the army, killing every one of the soldiers.

We jumped for joy and celebrated with the Israelites, praising the Lord at the top of our lungs.

Gabby appeared out of the crowd and took my hand. And then, without warning, we were once again in the presence of Dr. Manning.

Chapter 5

Bad News from Dad

When we arrived back at the library, I staggered in like I had just played two games of full-court basketball. It didn't help that Dr. Manning had taken us for hamburgers, fries, and milk shakes on the way home. I was tired before we indulged in fast food; now I could barely keep my eyes open. Who knew that going with my mom to the library could be so tiring?

Who knew that going with my mom to the library could be so tiring?

"Hey, kiddo," my mom said. "Did you have fun?"

I nodded.

"I'll be done in a few minutes. I told your

father we would pick up a pizza on the way home."

"All right." Though my stomach was full at the moment, I knew that by the time we arrived at the house I would be ready to eat again.

"Mom, where are the Bibles?"

She stopped typing and lowered her reading glasses as she looked at me. "You want to know where the Bibles are?"

"Yeah."

"Your father said he thought you might be coming down with something. I think he's right. Come here and let me feel your forehead."

"Mom, I'm not sick. I'm just curious." Gabby had said that on our next adventure we would learn about Jonah and the whale, so I thought I'd get a head start and surprise her.

On our next adventure we would learn about Jonah and the whale.

"Well then, Mr. Sanger, follow me, sir. We have a collection of wonderful Bibles for you to choose from."

My mom was right. There were rows and rows of them. They came in all sizes. Some were short and thick, others were tall and narrow. I ran my fingers across the spines of the books as I walked down the aisle. I had never been into old things. For instance, my mom had an antique chair and I couldn't stand it. The wood was dark and elaborate and the padding was covered with stitched roses. And it was so uncomfortable. *But it's an antique*, she would say, and whenever she said it her back straightened a bit. To me it was just plain old. So I surprised not only my mom but also myself when I discovered that the older the book, the more I seemed to be drawn to it. I quickly realized why. The older the Bible, the more detailed and wistful the artwork was. It seemed so alive, like the pictures in Dr. Manning's book. The Bible I checked out that evening was over one hundred years old and had two amazing pictures of Jonah and the whale— our next adventure.

We stopped and picked up an extra-large pizza for my dad and a large for me and my mom. My dad ate like a horse. When we arrived at the house he was taping a box shut.

"Honey," my mom said, "you're supposed to be emptying the boxes, not resealing them."

He shook his head, giving her a look I'd seen before.

"You're kidding, right?"

Again he shook his head. "The New York

Knicks just bought out my contract. We're moving back to the United States."

"When?" my mom asked.

"In a week."

"What?" I cried. "I like it here. Do we have to go?"

"I thought you'd be happy, Brett. I'll be playing in the Big Apple, alongside Al Harrington. Plus, it's better for our family because I'll be making a lot more money."

"I don't want to go. I want to stay here."

"It's not an option, bud."

I looked at my dad, and my eyes began to well. I ran to my room, swung the door shut, and plopped down on my bed, my arms wrapped around the old Bible that rested on my chest, my eyes boring a hole in the ceiling. After a few minutes I wiped my eyes, sat up, and turned to the book of Jonah. I hoped that by focusing on the amazing pictures I could take my mind off everything else. One was a painting of Jonah being swallowed by the *great fish*, as the Bible called it. The fish in the painting was a serpentlike creature, with a long, thin body and giant tail shaped like a palm frond. Its head was

"I like it here. Do we have to go?"

like that of a duck, with a long beak and bulging eyes. The sea was raging and the men in the boat—where Jonah had been moments earlier—were looking on with fear in their eyes.

My dad knocked on the door. "Can I come in, buddy?"

I wiped my nose and said, "Yeah."

He sat down on my bed. "I'm sorry. I know it's not easy to move around."

"It's just that I'm getting used to living here. I've made a good friend, and I don't want to leave."

"You're old enough to fly here on your own now."

"It's not like you're going to be gone forever. With both of your grandparents living here, you can come and visit often."

"You mean it?"

"Of course. In fact, your mom and I were just talking and we agreed that you're old enough to fly here on your own now. If you'd like, you can come back in a few months and spend a week during Christmas break. I know both sets of grandparents would love having you."

My mood dramatically changed. "Okay. I'd like that."

"Then it's a done deal," my dad said, and we

sealed it with a pinkie promise. "What are you reading?"

"An old Bible I checked out from the library."

"That's a cool picture," he said.

I nodded in agreement.

"Well, how about some pizza before it gets cold?"

"All right."

While we ate pizza, my mom and dad discussed what needed to be done during our last week in Israel.

"I'm going to give notice to the library in the morning. And then there's packing to do, utilities to cancel, mail to forward. It's going to be a very busy week."

My dad said he would be able to help. Though he was an official member of the Jerusalem team for seven more days, they wouldn't be playing any real games during that period, so it made no sense for him to participate.

"Do you think it would be okay if I hang out with Gabby and Dr. Manning?" I asked.

"Well, that's up to Dr. Manning. I'm sure he's a busy man. He's been so gracious with his time as it is."

"I'm sure he won't mind," I said.

"Well, we'll check with him in the morning."

I lay in bed that night thinking about what the next day would be like. I figured Gabby would be sad; or I hoped she would be—at least a little. I opened the Bible and examined the second painting of Jonah. In this painting, Jonah had been spit onto shore by the serpentlike creature, smoke streaming from the fish's nostrils. Jonah's body was muscular, though his beard was white and his hair long and thin. The sky in the background glowed like a distant flame. It was strange to think that in sixteen hours I would be experiencing the real thing. Once again, though I was extremely tired, I could barely sleep.

Chapter 6

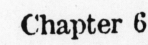

Jonah and the Whale

The next morning Dr. Manning agreed to keep an eye on me again, and Gabby was sad when she heard the news that I would be leaving. She was actually sadder than I expected

She was actually sadder than I expected her to be.

her to be, which had an effect on me. Her tears made me sad, too. When I explained that I would be back to visit, she perked up a little.

"Well," Dr. Manning said, "we have a lot of traveling to do in the next couple of days."

His enthusiasm was infectious. I immediately gathered up my wardrobe and quickly changed.

Jonah had boarded a vessel departing from

Joppa, a city adjacent to Tel Aviv and a short drive from Jerusalem. This time, to the surprise of all, *I* told the story. I did my best to be animated, but I wasn't a natural like Gabby. Jonah, I explained, was a prophet to whom the Lord had given the mission of traveling to the wicked city of Nineveh and proclaiming that in forty days the whole place was going to be destroyed. But Jonah feared and despised the people of Nineveh. He didn't think they deserved a warning. So he purchased a ticket and boarded a vessel heading in the opposite direction, out on the Mediterranean Sea. That's where the big fish entered the picture, as we would soon witness firsthand.

"This trip will be a little more complicated."

Dr. Manning pulled the Bentley into a beach parking lot. We trudged through the warm sand and sat down just shy of the water, the white foam of the waves sizzling as it dissipated just a few feet away.

"So here's what we're going to do," said Dr. Manning. "This trip will be a little more complicated than the previous two because it takes place over several days and the two of you only have an hour. So you're going to experience one event and then everything will become blurry. When the cloud is removed from your eyes, time will have elapsed and you will be in a different location."

This news made me a little nervous, but I didn't say anything.

"Are you guys ready?"

Gabby and I entwined our fingers, took a deep breath, nodded, and watched as the doctor opened the book and began to turn the pages.

"Take good care of her," he said to me with a wink. "See you two in an hour."

The next thing I knew, we were on the deck of a sinking boat. The waves were crashing around us and pulling us apart. A wave slapped me in the face.

"Gabby!" I screamed.

"I'm here, Brett!"

The boat swung one direction and then the next, the wood creaking, the sail clinging to the mast like a battle-torn flag.

The boat was taking on tons of water.

The boat was taking on tons of water. I sloshed forward toward Gabby and pulled her down so our backs were against the side of the boat. It didn't matter that we were sitting in several inches of water—it was the safest spot.

"Hey, you!" I heard someone yell. Several feet away from me, a sailor caught my eye.

I sat up straight and pointed at myself.

"Yeah, you," he hollered. "Give me a hand with this."

I jumped up and helped the man lift a barrel. Following the lead of the others, we hoisted it and released it into the sea. Men slid and fell as they tried to grab everything and anything of significant weight and toss it overboard in an attempt to keep us from sinking any further. The wind picked up speed, the sea growled, its waves punishing the vessel. I honestly didn't think Gabby and I were going to make it off the boat alive.

Suddenly a man yelled, "One of us must be responsible for this." He sloshed and stumbled across the deck and disappeared down a set of stairs. The sailors continued to throw the cargo overboard, and we helped as much as we were able. Not one person asked why we were on board. Then the man who had gone down below appeared again at the top of the stairs with something in his hand. Another man followed close behind him.

"You know how it goes," he yelled over the wind and crashing waves. "Each of you draw a straw! We'll find out who's responsible for nearly getting us all killed."

Everyone hurried over, drew a straw, and handed it back to the man Gabby and I now assumed was the captain of the vessel.

"Come on, you two!" the man called to us. "And hurry!"

We sloshed our way over to the captain. We each drew a straw and were relieved to see that both were short like the others. I wasn't quite sure what would happen to the poor fellow who got the long straw, but I knew it wouldn't be good.

"We can't let him die," I told Gabby.

The man who ended up with it was the one who had come up from below with the captain. While the sailors continued to throw stuff overboard, the captain demanded to know the man's name and why he was on board.

Just then a wave curled high above the boat and came crashing down upon us, leaving no one standing. Gabby and I ended up flat on our stomachs holding on to a pipe, the water rushing past us. Then we heard the doomed man shout, "My name is Jonah. I am a Hebrew and I worship the Lord, the God of heaven, who made the sea and the land. I'm the one who brought this on you. I have disobeyed the great God of Israel. Pick me up right now and throw me into the sea. Otherwise, you will all die with me!"

"We can't let him die," I told Gabby. We were glad to see that no one moved toward Jonah.

"Everyone grab hold of an oar," the captain yelled.

Gabby and I did as he said. The oars were long and thick, and Gabby and I, working together, could barely even move the wooden oar. Then something happened that I didn't think was possible—the storm got worse! The boat seemed to be dead in the water, and wood was splintering everywhere. The vessel was coming apart.

Two men grabbed Jonah, and he willingly gave in to them. "Don't let them do it, Brett!" Gabby pleaded, but there was nothing I could do.

The man on Jonah's left cried out, "O Lord, please do not let us die for taking this man's life. Do not hold us accountable for killing an innocent man, for You, O Lord, have done as You pleased." Then the men lifted Jonah and tossed him into the sea. The minute he hit the water, the sea sighed and relaxed. The wind quickly subsided and the boat steadied itself. Gabby and I jumped to our feet and watched in horror along with everyone else as a shark fin approached Jonah.

"Watch out!" I yelled, but Jonah didn't seem to hear me. Then the fish's head, which was covered with spots, appeared, opened its mouth wide, and swallowed Jonah in one piece. Its head plunged into the water and the fin disappeared. I don't know exactly how long its body was, but it was several moments before its tail rose out of the water and then splashed down. The creature was now completely out of sight.

"What was that?" I asked Gabby.

"I think it was a whale shark, but I'm not sure."

"Whatever it was, it was huge." The words were barely out of my mouth when the world suddenly became a blur. It took only a few seconds for us to go from a vessel in the middle of the sea to the sand where our adventure had begun. We were both cold and wet, like ice cream bars that had just been dipped in chocolate and peanuts, only the chocolate was saltwater and the peanuts were grains of sand. We scrambled to our feet just in time to see a huge wave approaching.

"I think it was a whale shark."

"Run!" I yelled.

The water was coming fast, dropping its

head like a charging bull. It crashed down at our heels and lifted us onto its back, depositing us a football field away from where we started.

"Oh, wow—look!" Gabby yelled.

We crawled away from the water like a couple of crabs on the run. I turned just in time to see the creature that had swallowed Jonah open its mouth and spit him out

Jonah was covered in green kelp.

on the shore. The memory of my father spitting up a piece of hot dog that had wedged itself inside his throat flashed through my mind. Jonah was covered in green kelp. He looked like he had been on the losing end of a Silly String fight. We were standing up to go to him when we were suddenly transported.

Dr. Manning couldn't wait to hear about our adventure. Apparently Jonah and the whale shark, as I now like to think of it, was one of his favorite adventures. We got some lunch at a local deli: ham, Swiss, lettuce, and tomato inside a pita. One thing I was beginning to realize about Israel was that just about everything was served inside a pita bread shell. As we sipped on Coca-Colas, we discussed what our next adventure would be. It would involve an overnight stay since it was so far away. I hoped my parents would go for it.

I figured the best time to broach the subject was at dinner, when I had my parents' undivided attention. Before I could say anything, my dad dropped another bomb on me.

"Brett, the Knicks would like me to fly in for a press conference tomorrow. Of course I'd love for you and Mom to be there with me—"

No way, I thought to myself. "Do I have to go? Can't I stay here? Dr. Manning has one more adventure planned for me and Gabby, and it involves an overnight stay. Dr. Manning said he would ask Mom in the morning if it would be okay if I went with them."

My dad looked at my mom. I could tell by the look on my mom's face that she was considering it.

"You didn't let me finish," my dad said. "What I was about to say is that I would like you to come along with us, but I'm going to leave that up to you. Your grandparents have already said you can stay with them until we get back. We'll only be gone for two days. When we get back, we'll finish packing and then the three of us will head back to the U.S. for good. I know I have dropped a lot on you in the past twenty-four hours, so it's okay if you want to stay."

"I want to go," I said, because I didn't want to disappoint my dad, "but I also want to stay."

"I understand. You don't have to decide right this minute. You can let me know in the morning."

"And what about going on an overnight trip with the Mannings if I decide to stay?"

"That's something your mom and I will need to discuss in private."

Choices:

✔ To see what happens if Brett chooses to fly with his parents to the press conference, continue with the next chapter.

✔ To see what happens if Brett chooses to stay, skip chapter 7 and go to chapter 8.

Chapter 7

Back to America

Though I really wanted to stay and go on the next adventure, I decided to go to the press conference with my parents. It was a hard decision to make, and I know it disappointed Gabby, but I felt like it was for the best. I dressed in warm clothes since it was about forty degrees colder in New York City. We took a taxi to the airport where we waited two hours for our plane to arrive. Apparently it was *coming* from New York City, where severe weather was delaying the departing flight. Sitting in the airport gave me a lot of time to think about what I had experienced over the past week.

I had thought of treasure as sparkling gold.

Until seven days ago, I had thought of

treasure as sparkling gold that could be bought or sold for a certain price. But the adventures that Gabby and I had taken together changed how I looked at treasure. Sparkling gold had been replaced by sparkling eyes, and monetary value had been replaced by what my mom liked to refer to as *schema*. You could put a price on reading about something, but you couldn't put a price on actually being there.

I had seen a boy not much older or stronger than me overtake a giant. I had watched an entire army be defeated without a single sword being drawn. And I had watched a shark swallow a man whole and then spit him out on the shore alive. David and Moses both had unreasonable faith, and God gave them victory. I can't say that Jonah exhibited unreasonable faith, but I reread his story with renewed interest.

> *David and Moses both had unreasonable faith.*

When Jonah landed on the shore, he stood up, shook himself off, and headed straight for Nineveh to carry out the mission God had given him. He declared the message of the Lord to the people, and they stopped their evil practices and called on the Lord. Then God, who is always merciful, forgave them.

After what seemed like forever, we finally boarded the plane. The one perk for waiting so long was that the airline let us have an extra soda pop and a free movie. I hardly noticed the movie; a better one was replaying in my head.

Suddenly the pilot's voice came over the loudspeaker, asking us to stay in our seats and buckle our seat belts. That's when I noticed the ride was beginning *We had just hit some bad weather.* to get a little rough. The plane jerked to the left and dropped suddenly before recovering. My mom was sitting between me and my dad and digging her nails into our arms. She hated flying even under the best of conditions.

"It's going to be all right, Mom," I said, trying to reassure her.

The lights flickered. I saw a bright flash of light outside the window, and then the cabin went dark.

The flight attendant tried to remain calm and tell everyone that the captain had everything under control, that we had just hit some bad weather and the lights would be back on in a moment. But then we saw her stick her head inside the cockpit. When she stepped out, she shouted, "Put your heads in your laps and brace for impact!"

A woman screamed and a baby wailed. Dad grabbed me and pushed me forward and down in my seat. I could hear both my parents praying and I joined them. "Lord, save us, all of us!" The adventures of the past few weeks flashed through my mind like a video in fast-forward. Two words were emblazoned on my thought track—*unreasonable faith*—and I repeated them over and over. Then it hit me: *If God could miraculously deliver David, Moses, and Jonah, can't He keep this plane from crashing?*

I held on to that thought, even as I felt the plane falling, being pulled toward the Atlantic Ocean as if it were a giant magnet. We were nose-diving. If the plane crashed, there was no doubt in my mind it would explode on impact. My dad leaned in my direction and told me that he loved me. Was this the end? *Unreasonable faith!*

A joyful shout rose up and filled the cabin.

And then just like that, the lights flickered on and the plane began to pull up and level out. A joyful shout rose up and filled the cabin; people hooted and hollered. The pilot's voice came over the loudspeaker, "I don't know how, but the plane's power has been restored, folks.

Let's all say a word of thanks to the Man upstairs. I know a miracle when I see one. Please keep your seat belts on just to be safe. We are still going to experience a bit of turbulence, but we should be on the ground in New York City in about twenty minutes."

I thought my mom was going to have a heart attack. She had to wear the oxygen mask that hung down from above her seat to steady her breathing. My dad held her in his arms. "Are you okay, buddy?" he asked me.

"I'm good, Pop."

I leaned my head back against my seat and thanked the Lord for saving us. I couldn't wait to get to New York and call Gabby to tell her what had just happened.

When I called Gabby the next day, she sounded happy to hear my voice. She listened closely as I told her about our near-tragic plane ride and how God had asked me to call on my unreasonable faith just as He had in our adventures.

"Were you scared?" she asked.

"Well, sure—very!" I answered. "But somehow I knew God would take care of us just like He did on the deck of that ship and when that nasty Egyptian tried to run over us with his chariot. I remembered how brave David was when he faced that giant, and I knew I had to trust God just as much to save us."

"Well, I'm glad He did save you, *very* glad. I can't wait until you come back for Christmas break," she said. "Who knows how many adventures are waiting for us!"

Chapter 8

Daniel, Shadrach, Meshach, and Abednego

It was a tough decision, but I decided to stay in Israel. My parents were totally cool with it. They even gave their permission for me to go out of town and stay the night in Babylon with Dr. Manning and Gabby.

It was dark when we got to Babylon. We had just enough time to eat dinner before settling down for the night. Dr. Manning had reserved two rooms: one for him and

It was dark when we got to Babylon.

Gabby and an adjoining room for me. Though I wouldn't admit it to the others, I was a little scared about being in a room by myself. I left the nightstand light on the lowest setting all night. It took me awhile to fall asleep, and I woke up several times. When the sun rose, I felt a little sluggish but was eager to see my friends.

Dr. Manning told us this day would be un-forgettable because we would experience so much in such a small amount of time. We dressed in our ancient-looking

"Do you know what the king dreamed?"

attire and headed toward the site where King Nebuchadnezzar's palace once stood. There was no time to waste. Dr. Manning turned to the stories recorded in the book of Daniel and then with little warning said, "Ready, set, go," and we were off.

"You're stalling!" I heard an angry voice say. "Tell me the dream and interpret it—or die!"

Someone shoved me. "Hey!" I said.

A red-faced man hovered over me and scowled. "Do you?" he demanded.

"Do I what?"

"Do you know what the king dreamed?"

"How would I know?" I asked.

"Somebody better figure it out or we're all going to die."

"Why don't you just ask him?" I said. Seemed reasonable enough to me.

"He won't tell us. He wants us to tell him what

he dreamed. And then he wants us to interpret it."

"But that's impossible," Gabby said.

"Exactly," the man said, doing a double take. "You're a girl."

"Yeah, so?"

"So, you belong with the women. Get me something to drink."

"I will not."

"You will, and you will do it now."

"No."

"Yes."

"No."

Disgusted, the man stomped off. I couldn't help but laugh. "You're a girl," I said to her.

She laughed. "Geniuses, these men."

We took a moment to look around us. We seemed to be inside a palace. Across the room from where we stood we saw a huge throne. A man we could only assume was the king was seated on it, scowling at the group of men kneeling before him.

"What you're asking, O King," one of the men said, "is impossible. No man can do this."

"I pay you all lots of money to read the stars and perform magic and predict the future and you cannot even tell me what I dreamed? Tell me now or die!"

"But, King, we cannot."

"Then you all shall die. Arioch, take these men away from me and put them to death—every one of them."

"Hey, wait a minute. I'm not with them. Let go of me."

"Let go of him," Gabby yelled. "Let go of him."

Chains secured my hands behind my back and wrapped around my ankles. I was being dragged away. By the time I had a chance to process what

"Then you all shall die." was happening, I found myself in a dungeon with a bunch of astrologers, magicians, and sorcerers. It was cold and the ground was wet. A rat scurried across the ground in front of me. Everyone around me was furious. "Nobody can fulfill that request," one man said to the other. "Who does he think we are? Mind readers?"

"Jailer!" I yelled. "I don't belong in here."

The jailer just laughed. "I don't make the rules, kid."

All of a sudden I was on dry ground and the sun was shining on me. Gabby threw her arms around me. "You're okay," she said.

"I'm sorry, son," Dr. Manning said. "I meant to turn one more page. The same thing that happened to you happened to me once. If my memory serves me right, the rats in the dungeon were huge."

"You got that right," I snapped back at him disrespectfully. I thought he was going to straighten me out, but I don't think he heard me. His eyes were glazed over; no doubt he was picturing those huge rats.

"This next part will be better," he said. "But I must warn you. The rats will be present once more just as you arrive, so be prepared."

Great, I thought to myself.

"The next hour is going to be a blur—literally," he said. "You guys are going to experience several incredible moments."

"On the count of three," he said. "One, two, three."

Instantly I was back in the dungeon, this time lying on my back in the water, a rat the size of a small cat sitting on my chest and staring into my eyes. I screamed. Yes, I screamed like a little girl, louder than was called for, and though everyone in my cell began laughing their heads off, the rat got the message and took off running. Just then the iron bars that held us in opened,

I screamed like a little girl.

and we were summoned back to the king. I realized as we were walking that a whole night had passed. When we reached the king's court there was a buzz in the air. Some guy named Daniel had not only told the king what his dream was but had interpreted it for him as well.

"Who is this Daniel?" a magician asked.

"He's a Hebrew," replied a man wearing a red robe and a red cone-shaped hat. "He was brought in here from Jerusalem after we besieged the city. He claims his God revealed the dream to him and interpreted it."

Everyone was ecstatic because their lives had just been spared. As for me, I just wanted to find Gabby. The palace was like a shopping mall, three levels tall with more than a hundred rooms. I went from room to room in search of her, opening door after door until I heard her voice cry out from a second-floor room. I hurried into the room, but it was empty. Racing across the floor, I pulled back the curtains at the window and looked down into a courtyard. There she was. Some man had her by the arm and was trying to cover her mouth with his free hand. Anger boiled up inside me, and a sense of courage I didn't know I had surged through me.

Without thinking, I leaped from the window, latched onto a palm tree a good five feet from the windowsill, and slid down it like a fireman. It was fortunate for me that it was a smooth skin palm and not the kind with the thorny fronds. I hit the ground hard, my knees buckling but not slowing me down. Gabby wasn't taking the man's aggression nicely, but I could see that she was no match for him.

Gabby wasn't taking the man's aggression nicely.

Neither Gabby nor the man had noticed me yet. I was tall for my age and strong. I charged at him like he was my last meal. Gabby saw me when I was about thirty feet away and bit down hard on his arm. He yelled as he released her and then raised his right arm to hit her, but I got to him first, delivering a blow that he would not soon forget. He was a few inches taller than me but skinny. I dropped my shoulder and buried him in the dirt.

"What do you think you're doing?" I yelled down at him as I jumped to my feet. He just stared at me in shock. "You never treat a lady like that! Never!"

I hurried over to Gabby. "Are you okay?"

"Yeah, just a little scared."

"Don't worry," I said. "I'll get you out of here."

The words were barely out of my mouth
when everything went blurry. Suddenly we
were standing at the base of a gold statue
that was as wide as a bus and seemed to
reach to the stars. We were surrounded by
men in purple and blue silk robes, wearing thick gold chains and glistening silver
rings. A short man clothed in humble attire
cried out: "According to the edict set forth
by King Nebuchadnezzar, when you hear the
sound of music, every one of you must fall to
the ground and worship the image of gold.
Those who refuse to do so will be thrown into
a blazing fire." Suddenly the sounds of horns
and flutes and harps filled the air and all the
people fell to the ground and began to praise
the image.

Gabby and I stood still, looking at each
other in disbelief. "Is this a joke?" Gabby
asked, laughing.

"I don't think so," I said, and immediately I
pictured God up in heaven looking down and
thinking to Himself: *Are you kidding Me?*

Looking around, I noticed three men who
were not bowing down. I nodded in their direction and they returned the gesture. A moment later I heard a group of men reporting
to the king that Shadrach, Meshach, and

Abednego had not bowed down along with everyone else. The king's face turned beet red, and he barked at the man who had shouted the edict on his behalf. "Bring Shadrach, Meshach, and Abednego before me at once."

The group of men who had ratted out the righteous fellows walked by me smiling smugly at each other. I should have kept my mouth shut and been happy that they hadn't noticed me and Gabby standing there, but I didn't. "Tattletales," I said.

"What did you say to us?" one of the men asked.

Before I could respond, Gabby said, "He called you big fat tattletales."

"Who are you kids and what are you doing here?"

"Who are you kids and what are you doing here?" I repeated.

"What?"

"What?"

"Stop copying me!"

"Stop copying me!"

By this time Gabby was laughing hysterically.

"Stop!"

"Stop!"

"Ugh," the man said, shaking his head. "Come, let us get away from these crazy children."

I was so busy poking fun at these three fools (I know kids are supposed to respect their elders, but please, the dudes were worshiping a gold statue) that I missed what the king said to the three men who wouldn't worship the gold image. I started listening closely.

"O King," I heard one of the three men say, "we will not worship the image, for we serve the one true God. So if you're going to throw us in the fire, do it. Our God will save us if He chooses to. But even if He doesn't, we will die worshiping Him and Him alone."

The king was so mad that when he yelled, spit flew through the air. "Bind these men with ropes from head to toe and heat the furnace seven times hotter than usual. I want you to throw their defiant bodies into the fire so I can watch the flames turn them to ashes."

"Our God will save us if He chooses to."

As luck would have it, I was summoned to get rope out of the king's underground storage room, which spooked me out because it was so dark inside. I was certain I heard a rattle coming from the far corner. Fortunately there was rope near the front. I grabbed as much as I could carry and hurried out. Gabby walked alongside me as I handed all of it to three Hercules' clones who tied up Shadrach, Meshach, and Abednego so tight there was no way their blood was able to flow through their veins. The three musclemen led the Lord's followers, who were waddling like penguins, to a huge furnace at the outer edge of the palace courtyard.

And that's when the most incredible thing happened. Before Shadrach, Meshach, and Abednego were even thrown into the furnace, their three escorts began to melt! It

It was like their skin was made of wax.

was like their skin was made of wax. The fire was that hot. By the time the Lord's followers had stumbled into the fire, the other men were liquid puddles of boiling skin.

Suddenly the king jumped up. "Are you seeing what I'm seeing?" he shouted. "Three men entered the furnace, right?" he said to his advisors.

"Certainly, O King," they replied.

"Then why are there four in there now?"

From a safe distance, Gabby and I saw exactly what the king saw. Gabby noticed it first. "Hey," she said, "I must be losing it. Who's in there with them?"

"Beats me," I answered, my jaw hanging low.

"Call them out of there," the king yelled. "Obviously these men really are servants of the Most High God."

We watched as the three young men emerged from the flaming furnace. All three seemed to be completely unharmed. With smiles on their faces, they made their way to the king. It was awesome!

Everyone, including Gabby and me, gathered around them. Not only were they unharmed, they didn't even smell like smoke. It was as if they had never been in the fire. "These men," I whispered to Gabby, "have unreasonable faith."

The three young men emerged from the flaming furnace.

Suddenly everything was a blur. Once it was crystal clear again, Gabby and I found ourselves in the palace kitchen standing in front of a long wooden table holding grapes, melons, strawberries, and fresh baked bread.

"Hurry, hurry," a lady said, placing in my hands a large plate filled to the brim with purple grapes. "Take these out to King Belshazzar." She turned to Gabby. "You come with me. You will dance for the king."

The king was easy to spot. He was seated at the head of the table and surrounded by many women. The diamond-studded crown on his head reminded me of those stupid cardboard crowns they give away at Burger King—except of course this one was real.

When I approached him, the king was speaking very loudly to a group of people gathered around him. He must have been telling a joke, because everyone was laughing it up like they'd never heard anything so funny.

"Grapes, Your Highness?"

He grabbed a handful without acknowledging me. I guess he thought he was on a roll, because he told another joke—also not funny—and once again everyone laughed hysterically. I suppose the fact that they had all been drinking wine worked in his favor. I began to walk away when he grabbed my arm and said, "Bring in the gold and silver goblets that my father took from the temple in Jerusalem when he conquered it, that we might drink wine in them." He howled with laughter and so did everyone else.

He told another joke—also not funny.

"Finally, some dancing girls!" he yelled, which was fortunate for me since the words that came out of my mouth at that very moment were,

"Dude, I think you've had enough wine."

One of the dancing girls tapped me on the shoulder as I was walking away. I didn't realize it was Gabby until she lifted the veil she was wearing.

"Where did you get those clothes?" I asked. She was wearing a shirt that barely reached her belly button and pants as thin as a bedsheet that swayed as she moved.

"Don't touch the goblets—they're from the Lord's temple!" she yelled, loud enough that I was able to hear her through the ringing of tambourines.

I took Gabby's words to heart, and though I didn't *touch* the goblets, I did pass on the king's wishes to have them brought out. I walked around the table, helping two other servants fill them with wine.

"Don't touch the goblets—they're from the Lord's temple!"

The king yelled, "Let us drink and sing praises to all of our gods." He held up his gold goblet. "To the gods of gold!"

Another person stood up and held high a silver goblet. "To the gods of silver!"

"To the gods of iron!"

"To the gods of wood!"

I was waiting for someone to yell out to the gods of dirt when the most amazing thing happened. The fingers of a human hand appeared out of nowhere and began to write words on the wall. Yes, you heard me right.

The king started freaking out. "What do they say? What do they say?

The king started freaking out.

Somebody tell me! You, servant boy, go find the enchanters, the astrologers, and the diviners. Tell them to come to me at once."

The room got really quiet. People were shaking with fear.

I grabbed one of the other servants. "Where are these guys?"

"Outside the palace main entrance, a hundred yards and to the left."

"Servant boy. . .go. . .go!" the king yelled.

I ran like I was being chased. I explained to the so-called wise men what had happened, and they followed me. They were as slow as turtles. I knew the king was probably having heart failure by now, but what could I do? These dudes were old.

After what seemed an eternity we finally arrived.

"What does it say?" the king asked anxiously. "Tell me. Tell me what it says and what it means. I will give riches and power to the one who tells me."

The men got excited. They may have moved like snails but they fought each other like lions, each jockeying for position in front of the wall. They examined the writing closely, their eyes green with greed, their mouths hanging open, eager to devour one another.

But they had no clue, no clue what it said or meant.

Then a woman spoke up. "Daniel, the Hebrew, interpreted dreams for your father, King Nebuchadnezzar. Surely he can tell you what the words mean."

The king looked at me and I looked at the servant who had given me directions before. In an instant I was off running again. I brought Daniel to the king. Daniel was young compared to the old goofs I had brought in before him. He couldn't keep up with me, but he didn't fall too far behind.

"Tell me what the words say and what they mean and I will give you riches and power," the king said.

Daniel was totally calm. He said to the king, "I'll read the words and interpret them because God has given me the ability to do so. But I don't want any of your filthy riches. Give them to someone else."

Daniel took his time studying the wall in front of him.

"What the words say is this: God is going to bring

"I don't want any of your filthy riches."

your reign to an end. He has examined you and is not pleased. Your kingdom will be ruled by the Medes and the Persians."

Disregarding Daniel's wishes, the king ordered someone to bring a purple robe and a gold chain for Daniel, and he declared him the third most powerful man in the kingdom. Of course, considering the words on the wall, that wasn't much of a prize.

The king got up to leave the banquet hall. He was halfway across the floor when a man jumped through a window, rushed toward the king, and stuck a sword through the king's heart. My jaw fell open. I couldn't have looked away if I'd tried. I stared as the king fell and died right there. No one came to help him, because all his people had rushed off to hide. Gabby buried her face in my shirtsleeve. I was turning to ask if she was all right when suddenly we were sitting on dirt and Dr. Manning was closing the book.

"That was some crazy hour, huh?" he said with a laugh.

I didn't know how Gabby felt, but I was exhausted.

"Did King Belshazzar have you run out and get the wise men?"

"Not just the wise men, but Daniel, too."

"Really? He had me fetch the wise men. But I wasn't as fit as you. I think he realized how tired I was because he sent another guy."

"I had to wear really skimpy clothes and dance for the king," Gabby said.

Dr. Manning looked at me sternly. "I thought you agreed to take care of her?"

"What was I supposed to do? I had a plate full of grapes stuffed in my face, and by the time I turned around, Gabby was gone."

Gabby turned to me and gave me her best puppy-dog eyes.

"Fair enough," he said, but I could tell he still wasn't happy with me.

"What's next, Grandpa?"

I looked at Gabby like she was crazy.

Dr. Manning picked up on my lack of enthusiasm. "I don't know. It's up to Brett whether you guys continue or not."

Gabby turned to me and gave me her best puppy-dog eyes. I looked at Dr. Manning. He knew I was defeated even before I agreed to set off on another adventure, because he was already opening the book.

"Well," he said, "you have two options. You can visit Noah and the ark, or Joshua and the wall of Jericho."

I told him I wanted to visit Joshua because that's who my dad was named after. Gabby said she wanted to visit Noah so she could pet the animals as they entered the ark. I wanted to go on an adventure that had a connection to my life but that I knew absolutely

We were at a real standoff.

nothing about. It's not that I knew that much about the adventures we had already been on, but I knew a little. I knew that David had defeated Goliath and that God had parted the Red Sea for the Israelites; and just about everyone had at some point in their lives heard of Jonah and the whale. I'd even heard about the handwriting on the wall. And I certainly knew the story of Noah's ark. But the story of Joshua and the wall of Jericho was totally new to me.

So Gabby voted for Noah, and I voted for Joshua. We were at a real standoff.

Choices:

✔ To see what happens if Brett and Gabby choose to visit Noah's ark, continue with the next chapter.

✔ To see what happens if Brett and Gabby choose to visit Joshua, skip chapter 9 and go to Chapter 10.

Chapter 9

Noah's Ark

We drove to the site where the ark was believed to have been built. I slept most of the way and I think Gabby did, too. I was excited to see the ark, but it seemed like the adventure itself

A boat, an animal entrance, and rain. Ho-hum, right?

might be kind of boring. I mean, what was there to it, really? A boat, an animal entrance, and rain. Ho-hum, right?

Not exactly.

Dr. Manning opened the book to the proper page, and just like that, we were standing beside a boat, trying to take in the enormity of it.

"This is the biggest boat I have ever seen," I

122 Bible Treasure Hunt

said, turning to Gabby. "Gabby?"

I felt like I was standing in the middle of Main Street at Disneyland, surrounded by so many strangers that it should have been easy to identify the one face that was familiar to me. But it never works that way. And this was certainly not a Disneyland crowd. If my mom had been present, she would have covered my ears. The muddy words that sprang from the people's lips splashed against my head like a water balloon and oozed down my eardrums.

"Excuse me," I said, trying to maneuver my way through the crowd. I soon learned this wasn't the time to be polite. I began to push through more aggressively, ducking to avoid the flying dirt clods that spattered against the wooden boat. I couldn't figure out if the people were angry or just having a good time. About a third of the people were throwing stuff at the boat, others were hurling insults at those inside, and the rest were laughing so hard they were holding their stomachs. And I noticed to my surprise that the women were acting as badly as the men.

If my mom had been present, she would have covered my ears.

It took me at least ten minutes to find Gabby.

"Hey, why did you run off without me?" I asked when I caught up with her.

"I'm sorry. I saw the animals and I couldn't wait to get near them. Did you see the zebras?"

"No, I was too busy looking for you."

"Everyone seems so mean," she said.

"I know."

"Oh, look at the giraffes. Aren't they beautiful?"

"I don't know if I would say they're beautiful. They're tall."

"Well, I think they're beautiful."

Gabby was so absorbed in the animals that she didn't even think to ask the most obvious question. So I did.

"Why is there a gigantic boat sitting in a grass field with no water in sight?"

"That's a good question."

"And why are they loading animals into it?"

"Another good question."

"Because Noah's an idiot," the man next to me grumbled. "He's a lunatic! Says God told him He's had enough of our wickedness. He plans to cover the whole earth with water. Look around and tell me what you see," the man said, making a sweeping gesture with his hand.

"The old guy's lost his marbles."

"Exactly—what water? He's been building this monstrosity for years, and now he's busy loading it up with animals. The old guy's lost his marbles."

I turned to Gabby and before I could even part my lips she said the words. "Unreasonable faith."

"Exactly," I said.

"Most of the animals must already be on the boat," Gabby said.

A pair of rhinoceroses walked up the long ramp, followed by a pair of sheep with thick wool coats. When the man following the sheep stepped inside, another man joined him and they began to tug at the ropes that were attached to the platform, slowly lifting the ramp.

As the ramp rose, I noticed that a cloud was beginning to scrape the top of a mountain a good distance away. I pointed it out to Gabby. By the time the ramp was halfway up, clouds were splattered across the sky. But we seemed to be the only ones who noticed.

A man standing near us bellowed, "You know the old man said anyone who wanted to could put their trust in God and come on board." Shaking his head, he slapped his knee and laughed heartily. "Yeah, right! Like anyone wants to be in that stupid boat with all those smelly animals!" He was still laughing as he disappeared into the crowd.

By this time the ramp was closed and we could hear a heavy wooden latch falling into place. And then it happened—the sky went from blue to gray in a matter of minutes. It was as if the clouds had been hiding behind the mountain preparing to attack. A sprinkle was soon replaced by driving rain, and then hail. I grabbed Gabby's hand and we ran to the nearest oak tree. Everyone began to seek shelter. There were very few trees, so we were all scrunched to-

A sprinkle was soon replaced by driving rain.

gether. Without warning, water began to trickle up out of the ground as well. Some people were still laughing. "Come on," they said, "a little rain never hurt anyone."

At that point, Gabby and I decided to crawl up into the tree. We went as high as we could go and still have some branches over our heads to soften the force of the hail. We made a little tent with what we could spare of our clothing. And we waited to see what would happen next.

The water was rising quickly, and people were beginning to panic, realizing that old crazy Noah might not have been so crazy after all. People screamed and ran toward the ark, pounding on it and screaming to be let in. The ark slowly began to lift and sway. Gabby and I held on to each other.

"Do you think we're going to die?" Gabby asked, her voice quivering.

I had already asked myself the same question. "No. We're going to be okay," I said, although our situation was looking pretty bad.

Animals began to climb up the trees, and birds began to seek shelter among the branches. It was getting a little crowded. This was good since the creatures stole a little of Gabby's attention away from the rising waters, but not so good was the risk of being bitten by a wild animal.

Abby cupped a tiny mouse in her hands. "Look," she said. "Look how cute he is."

I was not an animal person but I humored her nonetheless. "He's very cute."

"Well. What did you think?"

It took me a moment to realize that we had returned to Dr. Manning. Each trip seemed to be a little more absorbing and a little more difficult to return from.

She was still holding the tiny mouse.

"I thought we were going to die," I said.

Gabby quickly turned to me and said, "You said we were going to be okay."

"I was trying to make you feel better," I answered.

She shook her head at me and then opened her hands. She was still holding the tiny mouse.

"Where did that come from?" Dr. Manning asked.

"I was holding him when we were in the tree."

"In the tree?"

"Yeah, we climbed up a tree to escape the floodwater. This little mouse crawled up on my lap. I'm going to name him Noah."

"Name him? Don't name him. You can't keep him."

Dr. Manning's tone scared Gabby. "Why not?" she asked, sounding surprised.

"Because he's part of history. You can't bring anything back with you." He sounded more distressed.

"Why didn't I think to tell you?"

"But we bring back knowledge. You yourself said that the knowledge we bring back through our experiences is a priceless treasure."

"Yes, because true treasure is intangible. That mouse is tangible. You can't bring anything back that's tangible. It's my fault. I should have told you this." His eyes shifted away from Gabby. "Why didn't I think to tell you?" he asked himself.

"Define *tangible* for me," Gabby said. "And who says you can't bring anything back?"

"Something is tangible when you can touch it. And in this particular case, the Bible tells us."

Dr. Manning always had a Bible with him. He went to the car and retrieved it. I sat exhausted, wondering how Gabby had the energy to make such a fuss over the furry little thing.

Dr. Manning opened the Bible and read: " 'And the LORD said unto Noah, Come thou and all thy house into the ark; for thee have I seen righteous before me in this generation. Of every clean beast thou shalt take to thee by sevens, the male and his female: and of beasts that are not clean by two, the male and his female. Of fowls also of the air by sevens, the male and the female; to keep seed alive upon the face of all the earth.'" He closed the Bible.

"You see, the Lord only intended to save a specific number of animals. That mouse you are holding was not supposed to survive. He must be returned."

I knew that if we went back to the scene of the ark there would be little chance we'd make it to Jericho. I was just about to complain when my dad's voice suddenly crept into my head: *There are times when you have to man up, son.* I knew this was one of those moments. "Okay," I said. "I'm ready."

"It's not quite that simple," Dr. Manning said. "There's something you don't understand."

"What's that?"

"You can only visit a particular moment once. That's why I was unable to take Gabby on these trips. I had already been on all the adventures and couldn't go back, not even if I wanted to. To return, you would have to return to the exact moment that you left. And you would have to remain for an hour. I can't guarantee that there will be any dry ground available."

"I have a better chance of surviving."

"So what are you saying?"

"I'm saying that I can't put your lives at risk."

"So the mouse is going to remain here with us?" Gabby asked cheerfully.

Dr. Manning shook his head.

Gabby looked perplexed. "Then how is the mouse going to get back there?"

I already knew the answer to her question. "No," I protested. "I'm younger. I have a better chance of surviving."

"I can't let you take that risk, Brett."

He stood up, pulled his cell phone from his pocket, and walked several feet away to make a call. Gabby and I could hear that he was talking to her mother. When he wasn't looking, I took the mouse from Gabby.

When he got off the phone he told us that Gabby's mother was on her way to meet us since there was a chance he might not return. He reopened the storybook, found the page, and removed his glasses as he turned to Gabby. "Let me see the mouse, honey."

"Unreasonable faith, *sir. You coined the phrase.*"

She looked at me, and Dr. Manning's eyes shifted from hers to mine.

"Give me the mouse, son."

"With all due respect, sir, I can't do that."

"I appreciate your courage, Brett, but this is too risky."

"It's no more risky than when David took on the giant, or when Shadrach, Meshach, and Abednego refused to worship the golden image. They had unreasonable faith that God was bigger than the situation they were in. I believe that God is bigger than the situation I am about to enter. *Unreasonable faith*, sir. You coined the phrase."

Dr. Manning's shoulders slumped. "No, son, you've got to let me take the mouse back."

"Sorry, no," I answered, stepping back a few feet. I could feel the little mouse moving around in my closed hands.

Once Gabby realized that I was going, she said, "I'm going with you."

The doctor and I replied in unison, "No way!"

Dr. Manning walked toward me, still trying to convince me to let go of the mouse. Gabby, seeing that he was distracted, took the *Bible Treasure Hunt* book in her hands.

"Be safe, Brett! On the count of three!"

I took a deep breath, being careful not to squeeze the mouse.

"One, two, three."

The wind was howling. I set the mouse on a tree branch and then held on for dear life. The clouds growled and the rain raged. The sky was so dark it was hard to tell if it was day or night. I saw kids in trees and other kids and adults climbing a nearby mountain, the water rising in their wake. By my judgment, those of us in trees had less than an hour before the water

"Those of us in trees had less than an hour before the water reached us."

reached us; those on the mountain had maybe three hours. Two squirrels clung to my back and a crow nested in my hair. I swatted at the crow and he flew away; I tried to shake off the squirrels, but they were clinging to me as tightly as I was clinging to the tree.

I was soaked all the way through and starting to feel cold. The water was close to reaching my feet. The branches above me were thin. If I climbed any higher they would snap under my weight. I had maybe ten minutes before I would have to let go of the tree. I knew that to have any chance of treading water for an extended period of time I would have to remove my clothes; the weight of them would quickly pull me down. Removing the tunic was easy; removing the gown, though, was painful since the squirrels had dug their claws through the fabric and into my back. I undid the straps on my sandals.

For a moment, I almost laughed thinking of what I must look like stripped down to my boxers, shaking like an Eskimo and clinging to the tree like a panda bear. When the water reached my chin, I let go. The current yanked me to my left, and within moments the tree was no longer visible. The good

I could hear people above me crying.

news was that I was heading straight toward the mountain; the bad news was that the water was pulling me fast. I slammed into the mountain hard and slowly crawled up to escape the water below me. My head was throbbing, but the rain was pounding me so hard I didn't realize that blood was gushing just above my left eye. I somehow managed to crawl a little farther up the mountain. When I could go no farther I just lay there. I could hear people above me crying, but no one ventured down to help. I closed my eyes and waited for the water to consume me.

"Brett, Brett, wake up."

I could hear Gabby's voice, but I thought I was dreaming.

Gradually her face came into view. Dr. Manning was a blur. It looked like he was taking off his shirt. He dropped down beside me and I could feel the dry cotton press up against my forehead.

"Ouch."

"Try to relax, Brett," Dr. Manning said. "We need to stop the bleeding."

Gabby was visibly upset. "Is he going to be okay?" she asked.

"He's going to be fine. We just have to stop the bleeding and get him to a hospital."

"No hospital," I said. "Let's go straight to

Jericho. If we go to the hospital, we won't have enough time."

But Dr. Manning was adamant. "Nope, that's it. You're going to the hospital."

"But—"

It was Gabby's turn to join her grandfather in saying, "No way."

Gabby's mother ended up meeting us at the hospital, where I had to have thirty-eight stitches. Gabby and I rode home with her while Dr. Manning followed in his Bentley. This time I was the storyteller, painting the best picture I could of what had happened.

My parents were not due back from the United States until the next day, so Gabby's mom took me to my grandparents. I knew my grandma would freak out when she saw the bandage wrapped around my head. When she asked me, I told her the truth: I hit my head on a rock.

I was disappointed that we didn't get to visit Joshua in Jericho, but Dr. Manning said that would be our first stop when I came back to visit.

Chapter 10

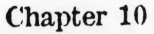

Joshua and the
Battle of Jericho

Gabby wasn't very happy about it, but I convinced her that it would be more of an adventure if we visited Joshua. After all, what could possibly happen on a trip

This would be a real adventure.

to Noah's ark? I mean, we'd see the boat; we'd pet the animals; and then we'd probably end up sitting around bored until the hour was up. This would be a *real* adventure.

The traveling part was beginning to be old hat to us. Dr. Manning opened the book, told us to have a good time, and we were off.

Instantlywefoundourselvesrunningalongwith a crowd of people headed toward a large tent. The fact that I couldn't keep up with Gabby was really

starting to eat at my pride. I was fast; I had always
finished first on skills day at my old elementary
school. But Gabby ate it up, too. As soon as we
reached the tent, she looked at me and asked
where I'd been.

"Very funny," I said.

We looked around and noticed that everyone seemed anxious to hear what the three men
in the center of the tent were saying.

There was a loud roar, and word soon reached
us in the back of the crowd. Two of the men had
spied on Jericho. Apparently the people of Jericho
were terrified of us.

The people of Jericho were terrified of us.

They had heard
how the Lord parted the Red Sea and wiped out
the Egyptian army.

"Who was the man in the center that the
two men were talking to?" I asked out loud to no
one in particular.

"What are you talking about, kid? That's
Joshua, of course," an old man close by offered.

"Of course," I said, looking at Gabby. "I told
you that was Joshua."

Gabby looked at me, perplexed.

I turned back to the old man. "Girls." I rolled
my eyes. "I tried to tell her it was Joshua and

she's like, 'No, it's not,' and I'm like, 'Come on, everyone knows that's Joshua.'"

Before Gabby could respond, everything became a blur. When things became clear again, we noticed it was morning. People were gathering their belongings and lowering their tents. Gabby and I offered to help carry an

"You mean the actual Ten Commandments?"

elderly couple's possessions, and they gladly accepted. Before we started walking, everyone was told to stay at least a thousand yards behind the ark of the covenant. I asked the elderly gentleman we were helping to tell me about the ark of the covenant. I expected to get an earful for asking such a question, but he was very nice and simply explained that it was a holy vessel that contained the Ten Commandments.

"The Ten Commandments?" I asked.

"Yes, you know, the Ten Commandments."

"You mean the *actual* Ten Commandments?"

He seemed a little perplexed at my lack of understanding but quickly recited them in an interesting manner I'd never heard of before.

"The simplest way I can put it is there are three do's and seven don'ts. You *should* have no other God but the Lord, honor your father and mother, and observe the Sabbath. You should *not* make an idol or bow down and worship one, use the Lord's name in vain, murder, commit adultery, steal, make false testimony, or covet."

Once again everything went blurry. Once again we were standing with the Israelites but in a different place. This time I could hear water raging nearby.

Joshua called everyone together. "Let me share the words that the Lord has spoken to me. The priests are to carry the ark before you. When they reach the Jordan River, they are to step into the water. When they do, the waters will halt, allowing everyone to cross on dry land like we did when we crossed the Red Sea."

The priests carrying the ark on their shoulders stepped toward the raging river. As soon as their feet touched the water, it began to pile up like a

"You can continue an adventure, but you can't redo it."

fleet of semitrucks, each slamming on its brakes at the same time, causing a massive pileup, halting traffic for hours. The ground instantly became dry. The priests stood in the middle of the river and waited for all of us to pass through. It was quite a sight to see.

Suddenly we were back in our own time, standing next to Dr. Manning.

"What happened?" I demanded. "We were right in the middle of the story."

Dr. Manning once again explained that we could only go for an hour at a time.

"Do we get to go back?" I asked.

"Of course," he said, turning the page. "You can continue an adventure, but you can't redo it."

In an instant we had assumed our places in line, waiting for our turn to cross the Jordan. As soon as everyone was safe on the other side, the priests continued across. The moment the last priest stepped out of the riverbed, the water came crashing down and swooshed past us.

"Awesome," I said to Gabby. "Totally awesome."

Once again everything went blurry. This time we were standing outside the wall of Jericho. I was amazed at how tall it was. The main gate was closed. Somehow I got the feeling no one in the city was happy to see us.

"Here is what the Lord has told us to do," Joshua said. "We are to march around the city in this order. A set of armed guards will go first, followed by seven priests blowing trumpets of rams' horns. The priests carrying the ark of the covenant will be next, with another set of armed guards following in the rear. The rest of us will follow."

Again things went blurry. I was beginning to get dizzy. Come to find out, six days had passed and the people had apparently marched around the city once each day. And on this, the seventh day, the people had already marched around the city six times for a total of twelve marches around the city. Gabby and I would soon find out that this was the final leg of the final march. After walking for just a short distance, I told Gabby I was pretty glad we hadn't been required to go around the city six times like everyone else. It was hot and dusty, to say the least—and boring because no one had much to say at that point.

We finally finished that final stretch, and the priests sounded the trumpets. We all snapped to attention as Joshua began to speak. "The Lord has given us the city. In a moment, I will give the signal and I want all of you—every man, woman, and child—to shout at the top of your lungs. And as I've said before, when we are inside the city, you must not touch the silver, gold, articles of bronze, and iron. Those belong to the Lord—no exceptions! Now. . .on

"The Lord has given us the city."

my count of three! One! Two! Three! Shout!"

I yelled at the top of my lungs and so did everyone else. The sound was so loud, I couldn't even hear my own voice. And then it happened—the huge city walls began to crumble inward. The shouting turned to cheers of victory as the men drew their swords, climbed over the debris, and flooded into the city. I didn't have a sword and wouldn't know what to do with one if I did, so we just stood there with the women, children, and older people. I grabbed Gabby's hand and we looked around to see what we could do. But that question was never answered because we were suddenly back with Dr. Manning. To be honest, I was a little disappointed. I had always wondered what it would be like to pillage a city! Ha! As if!

"I'm sad that it's all over," I said as the Bentley made its way through the streets of Jerusalem toward my grandparents' house.

"Me, too," Gabby said. "I'm going to miss you, Brett."

"I'm going to miss you, too," I said.

"Enough with the long faces," Dr. Manning said. "Brett will be back in a few months, and there are many more adventures in store for you."

When we were in front of my grandparents'

house, I lifted my overnight bag off the seat next to me and reached toward the front to shake Dr. Manning's hand. "Thank you, sir."

"No. Thank you, Brett. I was beginning to lose hope that I would ever meet you. Just remember, son, that when the Lord gave Solomon one wish, he didn't request gold or silver, but rather wisdom, and the Lord threw the gold and silver in as a bonus. Wisdom is the true treasure; gold is merely a prize."

"Wisdom is the true treasure; gold is merely a prize."

"With all due respect, sir, I would have to argue that true treasure is unreasonable faith."

The doctor smiled. "Son, I couldn't have said it better myself."

I stepped out of the car and closed the door. Gabby was waiting for me. She hugged me and kissed me on the cheek for the third time—not that I was counting.

"I'll see you in three months," she said. It came out more as a question than a statement.

"Yes."

"You promise?"

"I promise."

She hugged me one more time and then slid back into the car.

As I was walking up the cobblestone path, I heard the window roll down. And as the car pulled away, I heard Dr. Manning call out, "Unreasonable faith!"

And I responded the same, loud enough to bring my grandmother to the front door. She hurried out onto the porch and down the stairs to greet me.

"It was a trip I'll treasure forever."

"Did you have a good trip?" she asked.

I nodded and said, "Yep. It was a trip I'll treasure forever."

Start your own Bible adventure—
read through the whole Bible in a year.
It'll only take you about 20 minutes a day!

	Old Testament	New Testament	Wisdom Books
Day 1	Gen. 1–2	Matt. 1	Ps. 1
Day 2	Gen. 3–4	Matt. 2	Ps. 2
Day 3	Gen. 5–7	Matt. 3	Ps. 3
Day 4	Gen. 8–10	Matt. 4	Ps. 4
Day 5	Gen. 11–13	Matt. 5:1–20	Ps. 5
Day 6	Gen. 14–16	Matt. 5:21–48	Ps. 6
Day 7	Gen. 17–18	Matt. 6:1–18	Ps. 7
Day 8	Gen. 19–20	Matt. 6:19–34	Ps. 8
Day 9	Gen. 21–23	Matt. 7:1–11	Ps. 9:1–8
Day 10	Gen. 24	Matt. 7:12–29	Ps. 9:9–20
Day 11	Gen. 25–26	Matt. 8:1–17	Ps. 10:1–11
Day 12	Gen. 27:1–28:9	Matt. 8:18–34	Ps. 10:12–18
Day 13	Gen. 28:10–29:35	Matt. 9	Ps. 11
Day 14	Gen. 30:1–31:21	Matt. 10:1–15	Ps. 12
Day 15	Gen. 31:22–32:21	Matt. 10:16–36	Ps. 13
Day 16	Gen. 32:22–34:31	Matt. 10:37–11:6	Ps. 14
Day 17	Gen. 35–36	Matt. 11:7–24	Ps. 15
Day 18	Gen. 37–38	Matt. 11:25–30	Ps. 16
Day 19	Gen. 39–40	Matt. 12:1–29	Ps. 17
Day 20	Gen. 41	Matt. 12:30–50	Ps. 18:1–15
Day 21	Gen. 42–43	Matt. 13:1–9	Ps. 18:16–29
Day 22	Gen. 44–45	Matt. 13:10–23	Ps. 18:30–50

Day 320	Ezek. 20	Heb. 10:1–25	Prov. 18:18–24
Day 321	Ezek. 21–22	Heb. 10:26–39	Prov. 19:1–8
Day 322	Ezek. 23	Heb. 11:1–31	Prov. 19:9–14
Day 323	Ezek. 24–26	Heb. 11:32–40	Prov. 19:15–21
Day 324	Ezek. 27–28	Heb. 12:1–13	Prov. 19:22–29
Day 325	Ezek. 29–30	Heb. 12:14–29	Prov. 20:1–18
Day 326	Ezek. 31–32	Heb. 13	Prov. 20:19–24
Day 327	Ezek. 33:1–34:10	Jas. 1	Prov. 20:25–30
Day 328	Ezek. 34:11–36:15	Jas. 2	Prov. 21:1–8
Day 329	Ezek. 36:16–37:28	Jas. 3	Prov. 21:9–18
Day 330	Ezek. 38–39	Jas. 4:1–5:6	Prov. 21:19–24
Day 331	Ezek. 40	Jas. 5:7–20	Prov. 21:25–31
Day 332	Ezek. 41:1–43:12	1 Pet. 1:1–12	Prov. 22:1–9
Day 333	Ezek. 43:13–44:31	1 Pet. 1:13–2:3	Prov. 22:10–23
Day 334	Ezek. 45–46	1 Pet. 2:4–17	Prov. 22:24–29
Day 335	Ezek. 47–48	1 Pet. 2:18–3:7	Prov. 23:1–9
Day 336	Dan. 1:1–2:23	1 Pet. 3:8–4:19	Prov. 23:10–16
Day 337	Dan. 2:24–3:30	1 Pet. 5	Prov. 23:17–25
Day 338	Dan. 4	2 Pet. 1	Prov. 23:26–35
Day 339	Dan. 5	2 Pet. 2	Prov. 24:1–18
Day 340	Dan. 6:1–7:14	2 Pet. 3	Prov. 24:19–27
Day 341	Dan. 7:15–8:27	1 John 1:1–2:17	Prov. 24:28–34
Day 342	Dan. 9–10	1 John 2:18–29	Prov. 25:1–12
Day 343	Dan. 11–12	1 John 3:1–12	Prov. 25:13–17
Day 344	Hos. 1–3	1 John 3:13–4:16	Prov. 25:18–28
Day 345	Hos. 4–6	1 John 4:17–5:21	Prov. 26:1–16
Day 346	Hos. 7–10	2 John	Prov. 26:17–21

If you enjoyed

Bible Treasure Hunt

be sure to look for these other great Bible
resources from Barbour Publishing!

The Complete Guide to the Bible
7" x 9½", Paperback, 512 pages, $19.99
ISBN 978-1-59789-374-9

500 Questions & Answers from the Bible
6" x 9", paperback, 256 pages, $9.99
ISBN 978-1-59789-473-9

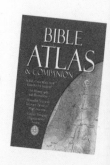

Bible Atlas & Companion
8" x 10", paperback, 176 pages, $9.99
ISBN 978-1-59789-779-2

Available wherever Christian books are sold.